Card Games for Kids

36 of the Best Card Games for Children and Families

***

Lindsay Small

Creator of
www.ActivityVillage.co.uk
Keeping Kids Busy

For "Grandpa",
who loved a good family card game

Table of Contents

Introduction

Sometimes in these days of computers, game consoles, smart phones, tablets and other expensive toys we forget that a simple pack of cards (or two) can provide hours of fun.

Cards are inexpensive, easily portable and endlessly adaptable. Families can enjoy a game together, kids can play in groups on their own, and a solitary child can while away the hours playing solitaire games, practising shuffling and dealing, or building card houses.

Card games also build all sorts of skills. Younger children will encounter number recognition, sorting problems, fine motor skills. Older children will start to use their strategic thinking skills and can benefit from watching (and trying to remember) the cards that other players put down or play.

So get the cards out and have a go! There are 36 games in this book to choose from, and I've tried to give an indication of appropriate ages (starting with games that the youngest children can enjoy and working up in age).

One more thing. If you are looking for games that will be enjoyed by all ages from kids up to grandparents, that will break the ice with a group that doesn't know each other well, and that will get people giggling, have a go at Pig (page 8) or Knock (page 44). These are personal favourites that my family returns to again and again.

Memory

Also known as Concentration, this card game is an old stand-by which can be adapted for all ages and abilities of children and is great for improving concentration and memory skills.

Number of Players: 2+ (but see Solitaire version below)

Age Range: 4+

Type of Game / Skills: Memory skills

Cards: One standard deck of cards, adapted as appropriate for age and ability (see below). You can also use pictorial cards, learning cards (for colours, numbers, alphabets and so on), or make cards particularly appropriate to your child's interests and hobbies.

Aim: To collect the most cards

Instructions: Select a number of pairs of cards appropriate to your child. Younger children could start with just 3 or 4 pairs, laid into a grid. Older children can use the whole pack of 52.

Shuffle, and spread the cards face down on the table between the players. You can sweep them into a random arrangement, or lay the cards out in grid form; the latter makes it easier to remember where cards are placed.

The object of the game is to find matching pairs. Players take it in turns to turn over 2 cards. Let all the players see them and study them. If they are not a matching pair, try to remember what and where they are, then turn them back over. Play then passes to the next player. If they *are* a matching pair, the player that turned them removes them from the table and keeps them, and then has another turn.

When all cards have been removed from the table, each player counts up the number of cards they have collected. The player with the most cards is the winner.

Variations:

Play a solitaire version: Older children can count how many "turns" it takes them to complete the game, and try to beat their record. Younger children may find it more helpful to have a pile of buttons and two cups. Move a button from one cup to the other for every "turn" and see if they can complete the game before all the buttons have been moved across.

Leave an odd card out: You can make the game a little harder for older children by leaving one card without its pair.

Card Bingo

This is a simplified Bingo game and you can play it with a big group of children. It helps to have an incentive such as a packet of sweets so that you can hand out a small reward at the end of each round!

Number of Players: 3+ (with an adult or older child to act as "caller")

Age Range: 4+

Type of Game / Skills: Number recognition

Cards: One standard deck of cards for up to 5 players, two decks for more players. Divide the packs up into red and black cards.

Aim: To turn over all your cards.

Instructions: The caller deals each child five cards from either the red or black half of the pack, face up in front of them. Now she turns over the other half of the pack one at a time, calling out the number. If a player has the same number, he turns that card face down. When all five cards are face down, he calls out "Bingo!" and wins a small prize.

Old Maid

This is a popular and easy card game for three or more children. It makes a good starter card game for kids. Also called "Pass the Lady".

Number of Players: 3+

Age Range: 5+

Type of Game / Skills: Luck

Cards: A standard deck of 52 cards is used, but with one of the Queens removed. This leaves a pair of Queens in one colour and a single Queen (the "old maid") in the other.

Aim: To avoid being left with the "old maid"!

Instructions: All the cards are dealt, face down. It doesn't matter if some players end up with more cards than others.

The players sort their cards, keeping them hidden from all other players. Anyone holding pairs of matching cards, with the same number or picture, should put them down on the table, face up. If anyone has three matching cards, he only puts down one pair and keeps the spare card. If anyone has four matching cards, he puts down two pairs.

The player to the left of the dealer then fans his remaining cards in his hand so that he can see them all, keeping them hidden from the other players. He offers them to the player on his left, who cannot see them, but takes a random card from the fan. If the card she picks matches any she already has, she puts down the pair. If not, she keeps it in her hand. Then, she, in turn, fans her cards and offers them to the player on her left.

This continues until all the cards have been put down in pairs, except the Old Maid, which is left alone and cannot be paired. The person left holding this card loses the game.

Variations:

Le Vieux Garcon: This is the French version of the game, and translates to "Old Boy" instead of "Old Maid". The Old Boy is the Jack of Spades. All

the other Jacks are removed from the deck and
the game is played as before.

Pig

This is a brilliant starter game for children, who enjoy the rhythm (once they get the hang of it) and the silliness of it all. It is one game that even the youngest child doesn't seem to mind losing, which makes it a real winner, and it is a great game for mixed ages! The game is similar to My Ship Sails (page 28).

Number of Players: 3+ (and up to 13 using one pack of cards)

Age Range: 5+

Type of Game / Skills: Luck, concentration

Cards: Standard 52-card deck

Aim: To collect four of a kind, or notice someone else do so!

Instructions: For each player, take four of a kind out of the deck. Put aside the rest of the cards. If you are playing with younger children, try to make sure that the cards are as different from each other as possible. For example, if you were playing with 3 players you might choose the 4s, 8s and Queens. Shuffle your chosen cards well.

Deal the cards face-down so that each player has four. Now each player looks at their hand and sorts the cards out. The aim of the game is to collect four of a kind, at which point you quickly, and quietly, put a finger on your nose. If you see another player put a finger on their nose, you must do so too (regardless of whether you have 4 of a kind or not). The last player to put a finger on their nose gets a letter - first P, then I, then G.

To play, decide which cards you want to collect then choose a card to discard and put it, face down, on the table in front of you. When everyone has a card on the table, simultaneously pass your card to the player on your left and then pick up the card which has been passed to you. Try to establish a rhythm - it can help if an adult says "down - pass - pick up, down - pass - pick up" to keep everyone going!

The first player to reach "P-I-G" is the loser. If you want a longer game, try playing with D-O-N-K-E-Y instead.

Snap

Snap is popular, noisy and liable to go on forever! It is a fast game for the whole family, requiring quick reflexes and sharp observation.

Number of Players: 2+

Age Range: 5+

Type of Game / Skills: Noisy, physical

Cards: Special snap cards are easy to find, although an old, standard deck can also be fun to use. Use two decks for more than three players.

Aim: To win all the cards.

Instructions: Deal out all the cards, face-down. Players don't look at their cards, but place them in a stack in front of them, face down.

To begin, the player to the left of the dealer takes his top card, turns it over and places it face up next to his own pile. The next player does the same, starting a pile of his own.

Continue until a player notices that two cards on top of any of the face-up piles are the same. Shout "Snap!" The first to do so receives all the cards in both of the matched piles and adds them to the bottom of his face-down pile. The game then continues, with the person to the left of the winner continuing play.

If, at any point, a player runs out of face-down cards, he simply overturns his face-up pile and starts again.

If two players shout "Snap!" at exactly the same time, they form a snap pool, with the two matched piles of cards placed together, face-up, in the centre. Play then continues as normal, until someone turns up a card which matches the top card in the snap pool. Whoever then shouts "Snap pool!" fastest takes the whole pool.

If a player incorrectly calls "Snap!" at any point, he should pay every player one card from his face-down pile.

If a player runs out of both face-up and face-down cards, he is out. The winner is the player who ends up with all the cards.

Variations:

Easy Snap: Extremely good for younger children, this variation of the game has only one central, face-up snap pile. The players each add a new card to the snap pile until the top card matches the one beneath it. The first player to shout "snap" takes the whole central pile and adds them to the bottom of his own face-down stack. If a player runs out of cards, he is out. The winner is the player who ends up with all the cards.

Speed Snap: This is a very fast version of the game, with everyone turning their cards over at the same time, instead of in turn.

Slapjack

This is an easy card game, suitable for very young children, but it can get wild and start off a few arguments so we have tended to avoid it! You might want to supervise young children. Nevertheless is remains a popular game for many.

Number of players: 2 to 5

Age: 5+

Type of Game / Skills: Physical

Cards: Standard deck

Aim: To win all the cards

Instructions: Deal the cards out completely, face-down - don't worry if the numbers are uneven. The player to the left of the dealer starts by turning the card on the top of his pack face-up in the centre of the table. Play continues with each player adding a card to the face-up pile, until somebody turns up a Jack, at which point all players try to be the first to "slap" their hand over the stack. Whoever gets their hand there first takes the pile and adds it to the bottom of their pack.

The player to their left starts a new face-up pile, and play continues.

If you lose all your cards you have one more chance to stay in the game, by slapping the next Jack that appears. If you miss that one, you are out for good!

The last person in is the winner.

Muggins

This is a fun game for a group of same-age younger children, or a group of children and adults. It doesn't work well with mixed ages of children as the older kids will tend to play too carefully and not to make mistakes, and it's the mistakes which make it fun! It is a good introduction to the more complicated sequencing games for older children later in this book.

Number of players: 4 to 6

Age: 5+

Type of Game / Skills: Noisy, sequencing

Cards: One standard deck. Ace is low.

Aim: To get rid of all your cards

Instructions: Deal out the cards to the players as follows:

* 4 players get 12 cards each and 4 cards are placed face-up in the centre as "Mugginses"

* 5 players get 10 cards each with 2 Mugginses

* 6 players get 8 cards each with 4 Muggineses

Players don't look at their cards but stack them neatly face down in front of them.

The player left of the dealer takes the top card from his stack and turns it over, placing it face-up nearby. The object of the game is to get rid of your cards by building them onto other face-up cards, either up or down.

For example, if there is a 7 face up on the table, you could build onto it with either a 6 or an 8. As an Ace is the lowest card you can only build onto it with a 2, and as a King is the highest card you can only build onto it with a Queen.

At each turn, a player looks at the newly-turned over face up card and first tries to place it on one of the Mugginses. If he can't (and only if he can't), he looks at the other players' face up piles to see if he can place it on one of them. If there is more than one card that he can build on, he has to choose the player nearest on his left. If he can't place his card anywhere, he leaves it where it is and says "Pass", and play passes to the next player on his left.

If a player is caught making a mistake, everyone calls out "Muggins!" and give him one of their face-down cards to add to his face-down pile. If a player runs out of cards in his face-down pile, he turns his face-up pile over and starts again.

When you manage to place your last card, you declare victory!

Chase the Ace

This is a simple game for a large group of youngsters – up to 8 or at a pinch 9 or 10. It helps children to learn about "higher" and "lower" and is exciting to play. It is also a good early introduction to Pontoon (page 96).

Number of players: 4 to10

Age: 6+

Type of Game / Skills: Numbers, higher / lower

Cards: One standard deck. Ace is low. You will also need three counters for each player. If you play with sweets as counters, the winner will have a treat!

Aim: To avoid having the lowest card and to be the last in the game.

Instructions: Deal one card to each player, face down on the table. The player left of the dealer picks up his card and looks at it. If it is a King, the highest card, he puts it face up in front of him. Otherwise he decides if he likes his chances with it (that is, it is a high card) or doesn't. If he does, he puts it face down in front of him and says "stick". If he doesn't, he swaps it with the player on his left.

Play continues like this around the table, with each player deciding whether to "stick" or "swap". When play comes round to the dealer he can choose whether to "stick" or swap his card with the top card of the remaining pack.

All cards are now turned up, and whoever has the lowest card puts one counter into the centre.

If two or more cards are the same rank, the lowest card is decided according to Bridge rules, where Spades are the highest followed by Hearts, Diamonds and Clubs. So the Ace of Hearts would beat the Ace of Clubs.

Beggar My Neighbour

Beggar My Neighbour is one of the all-time favourite children's card games. It is an exciting game of luck, best played to a time limit to prevent frustration.

Number of Players: 2 to 6

Age Range: 6+

Type of Game / Skills: Luck

Cards: For two or three players, one standard deck of cards can be used. Any more than three players will require two decks.

Aim: Not to be the first to run out of cards

Instructions: All the cards are dealt, one by one, around the group, until there are none left. It does not matter if some players have more cards than others. Each player collects his cards in a face-down pile and does not look at them.

To start, the person to the left of the dealer places his top card face-up in the centre. Then the game moves around clockwise, with each player adding one card to the central pile until someone turns up an Ace or a Jack (Knave), Queen or King – the Court Cards. If a player turns up one of these cards, the next player then has to "pay a penalty" of a certain number of cards onto the pile as follows:

- An Ace - four cards
- A King - three cards
- A Queen - two cards
- A Jack - one card

If at any time during the penalty a new Court Card is turned up, the previous payment is cancelled and the next player along pays the new penalty.

When a penalty is completely paid (without being interrupted by a new Court Card), the player who started that penalty off picks up the central pile and adds it to the bottom of his pack. He then starts the next round.

When someone runs out of cards the game is over. If you want, you can give each remaining player a score by counting the number of cards they have left in their hand. The one with the most cards wins.

Example Game:

Player 1 puts down a 5. Player 2 places an Ace. Player 3 puts down a 4, 7, 9, 2. Player 2 wins the pile. Player 2 starts the next round by placing a Queen. Player 3 puts down a 9 and another Q. Player 4 puts down a 2 and a 5. Player 3 picks up the pack. And so on.

Menagerie

Be prepared for a lot of noise with this card game, which is also known as "Animals". Great fun!

Number of Players: 4+

Age Range: 6+

Type of Game / Skills: Noisy!

Cards: Two standard decks

Instructions: To start, each player chooses an animal name. The names you choose will depend on the ages of your children. Younger kids might learn to play with simple farmyard animals such as cow and horse. Older children might progress to much trickier creatures like the Pygmy Hippopotamus or Amazonian Umbrellabird! They then write these names onto slips of paper, which are folded up and shaken about in a hat or box. Each player then takes out a slip of paper and whichever animal they have selected is theirs for the rest of the game.

All players should learn the names of all the animals, not merely their own.

Next, all the cards are dealt clockwise and kept face down – don't look! It doesn't matter if the number of cards given to each player is unequal.

The player to the left of the dealer turns his top card over to start a face up pile next to his face down pile. Every other player does the same in turn, continuing around the circle. When a player notices that another player's face up card is of the same rank (that is, the same number or picture) as his, he has to shout out the name of the other player's animal three times. The first player to shout correctly wins the other player's face up pile, which he adds to the bottom of his face down pile.

If a player calls out the wrong name, he gives all his face up cards to the player whose name he did shout.

The winner is the player who manages to collect all the cards.

My Ship Sails

This is an easy card game for kids of all ages (from about 6 up) which is best and most exciting when played at high speed. The game is similar to Pig (page 11).

Number of Players: 4 to 7

Age Range: 6+

Type of Game / Skills: Luck, concentration

Cards: One standard deck of cards

Aim: To collect a hand of one suit

Instructions: Deal seven cards to each player, one at a time and face-down. The rest of the deck is not needed.

The aim of the game is to try and collect seven cards from the same suit (eg seven spades). Keeping the cards hidden, the players sort their cards by suits and decide which suit to collect. They may change their mind as play progresses.

Then, each player puts an unwanted card face down on the table and slides it to the player on the right, who picks it up. Try to do this in a rhythm so that all players are passing and picking up at the same time. Continue until one player's hand is all one suit. He shouts "My ship sails!" and wins the game.

Go Fish

Go Fish is a card game of chance and skill for two or more players. Younger children will just enjoy the excitement of it; older kids will begin to learn to try to memorize what cards the other players have. It is also a great introduction to more "grown-up" games such as rummy and whist.

Number of Players: 2+

Age Range: 6+

Type of Game: Luck and Skill

Cards: Either a standard deck or a special "Happy Families" pack can be used.

Aim: To put all your cards on the table in sets.

Instructions: The dealing depends on the number of players. If there are two or three, each player is dealt seven cards. If there are more people taking part, deal five per player. The remaining cards are placed face down in the middle to form the fish pile.

The players then have to sort their cards into groups of the same number or picture (i.e. a group of fives; a group of Queens), making sure not to show any other player their hand. Then, to start, the person to the left of the dealer asks any other player for cards of any one of the groups he holds in his hand. For example, if he has two Kings, he may ask the player opposite him for Kings. If that other player any Kings, he must hand them over. The "requester" can then go on asking the same player for more cards until the player does not have the cards he wants.

A player who does not have the cards he is asked for tells the requester to "Go Fish". The requester then has to take one card from the fish pile and the person who told him to "Go Fish" becomes the new requester.

Any player who collects all four cards of a set – for example, all four Jacks - puts them face down in front of him.

The winner is the first person to have nothing left but a collection of complete sets. If two people run out of cards together, the player with the most sets wins the game.

Example Game:

John asks the player on his right, Annabelle, for Aces. She hands over two Aces. He asks her for 5s. Annabelle says "Go Fish". John takes a card from the central pile. Annabelle asks the player opposite her, Mike, for 3s. He hands one over, and Annabelle puts four 3s down on the table. She then asks Mike for 9s. He hands over one 9. She asks him for Queens and he says "Go Fish". She takes a card from the central pile and it is Mike's turn to request cards.

Rolling Stone

This card game for kids can be fun but very frustrating: just when you are about to win, you can find yourself right back at square one! It is a good introduction to more difficult sequencing games.

Number of Players: 4 to 6

Age Range: 6+

Type of Game / Skills: Luck

Cards: If there are six players, one standard deck with the twos removed. If there are five players, twos, threes and fours removed. If there are four players, twos, threes, fours, fives and sixes removed.

Aim: To get rid of all your cards first.

Instructions: Deal eight cards face-down to each player.

The players sort their cards by suit and then the player to the left of the dealer plays one card face-up. The next player then has to play a card which is of the same suit. Play continues until a player cannot place a card, at which point they have to pick up all the face-up cards and add them to their hand. They then start the next round with one of their cards of a different suit. The winner is the player who runs out of cards first.

Sequence

This game is easy to learn, making a good starter card game for younger kids, but nevertheless requires concentration and patience.

Number of Players: Best with 4 to 5 but it is possible to play with as few as 2

Age Range: 6+

Type of Game / Skills: Luck, Sequencing

Cards: One standard deck. For younger children you could remove the picture cards and run each sequence from 1 (Ace) to 10.

Aim: To be the first to get rid of all your cards.

Instructions: In this game, cards are ranked in numerical order: 2, 3, 4, 5, 6, 7, 8, 9, 10, Jack, Queen, King, Ace, with Aces high. Cards in order and of the same suit make up a sequence.

To start, the whole deck is dealt clockwise around the group, face-down. It doesn't matter if the cards are unequal.

The player to the left of the dealer places his lowest card face up on the table (not necessarily a 2).The player who has the next card/cards in the sequence plays it/them. Play continues until the Ace of that suit is reached. Then, the next sequence is begun by whoever played the last card, starting with his lowest card.

If at any time a player plays a card that cannot be followed (when the higher cards in that sequence have already been played), he gets another turn. The winner is the player who is the first to get rid of all his cards.

Variations:

Rounds: This game can be lengthened by playing in rounds. To do this, each player starts with ten counters and a number of rounds is agreed upon. Then, every time someone wins a round, the losers pay him one counter for every card they still hold.

The ultimate winner of the whole game is the person with the most counters when the chosen number of rounds has been completed.

Sevens

Also known as Card Dominoes, Parliament or Fan Tan, this is an exciting card game which is simple for children to learn quickly. One of our family favourites!

Number of Players: 2+

Age Range: 6+

Type of Game / Skills: Sequencing

Cards: Standard 52-card deck.

Aim: To be the first to get rid of all your cards.

Instructions: The entire pack is dealt face-down. Players then sort their cards into sequences in each suit. The player who holds the 7 of Diamonds starts by placing this card in the centre. The game then continues clockwise, with each player, if they can, adding a diamond card to the sequence. They can build up (8, then 9, then 10 etc) or down (6, then 5, then 4 etc). Cards are placed on either side of the 7 to form a row.

In his turn, a player can also start a new sequence in a different suit by placing any of the other 7s below the 7 of diamonds so that a new row can be built in that suit. If a player can do neither, he simply skips a turn. The winner is the first player to use up all his cards.

Play or Pay

Here's another sequencing game, a little different from the previous ones. My children liked it because of the addition of counters!

Number of players: 3+

Age: 6+

Type of Game / Skills: Sequencing

Cards: Standard deck of cards. You will also need a large stack of counters, divided equally between the players. Aces are high.

Aim: To get rid of all your cards.

Instructions: Deal all the cards. Player to the left of the dealer begins by placing any card face up on the table. The player to their left must follow with the next highest card, or put a counter into the centre if they cannot. Continue until all 13 cards in the suit are on the table (continuing past the King with the Ace, 2 and 3 and so on.). The player who puts down the last card in that suit begins the next sequence with any card from his hand. The winner is the first to put down all his cards. He takes all the counters from the centre of the table!

Snip Snap Snorem

This is a popular - and noisy - card matching game, suitable for younger children and mixed age groups.

Number of players: 3+

Age: 6+

Type of Game / Skills: Noisy, matching, sorting

Cards: Standard deck of cards

Aim: To get rid of all your cards.

Instructions: Deal the cards out completely, face down. Players sort the cards in their hands by rank.

The player to the left of the dealer starts by placing any card down on the table. The next player looks to see if they have a card of the same rank. If they do, they place it down on top of the card, saying "Snip". If they have another card of the same rank, they place it down too, saying "Snap". If they don't, play passes to the next player, and so on. Whoever places the final card of that rank says "Snorem" and wins the right to start the next round with the card of their choice. Children will soon learn that it is best to lead with a card in which they have more than one of a kind.

Stealing Bundles

Also known as Stealing The Old Man's Bundle, this unpredictable game is very popular with kids, who love being able to steal each other's cards! It is an early version of Casino.

Number of Players: 2 - 4

Age Range: 6+

Type of Game / Skills: Luck

Cards: Standard 52-card deck

Aim: To have the biggest "bundle" at the end of the game

Instructions: Each player is dealt four cards, which are kept separate and face-down. Then, another row of four cards in put, this time face-up, in the centre. The rest of the cards are put aside.

The player to the left of the dealer has first turn. In each turn he does one of three things.

1. If he has a card which is of the same rank (ie: twos, Queens) as any of those in the centre, he can "steal" the centre card (or cards) and put it face-up with his own, in front of him, in a stack. This is his "bundle". If he wins more cards in future turns, they all go onto the top of this bundle, with only the top card showing.

2. If he has a card which is of the same rank as the top card in someone else's "bundle", he can steal their bundle!

3. If he has no cards which match the central ones or another's bundle, he "trails", putting one of his own cards face-up in the centre.

When everyone has played all four of their original cards, they are dealt four new ones and the game continues.

When all the cards have been dealt and played, the player with the most cards in their bundle wins.

War

War makes an easy introduction to card playing for kids without too many rules to complicate the game.

Number of Players: 2 (although 3 can play with our variation, below)

Age Range: 6+

Type of Game / Skills: Luck

Cards: Standard deck of 52 cards

Aim: To win all the cards

Instructions: Deal out the cards and keep them face down. Player must not look at their cards.

Both players turn over the top card in their piles and put them face-up in the centre. Whoever has turned over the higher ranking card, never mind which suit, picks up both cards and puts them at the bottom of his pile.

Continue in the same way until two cards of the same value (eg two 4s) are turned over at the same time. This constitutes "War". Both players then take two more cards and put one face-down on top of the card they have already placed in the middle, and one face-up. Whoever puts down the higher ranking face-up card wins all six.

If, of course, two more same-ranking cards are put down, the state of "War" continues until there is a winner.

The game is won by the player who manages to collect all the cards.

Variations:

War for Three: This is nearly the same as War (for two), except that the last card in the deck is not given out, to make sure that all the players have the same number of cards. Then, if two cards of the same rank are turned up, all three people have to go to "War".

If, however, three cards of the same rank are turned up, the players play "Double War", where everyone puts two cards face-down in the centre and one card face-up. If the cards happen to match, they continue with "Single War".

Trumpet

The great thing about Trumpet is that it teaches children about "tricks" and "trumps" in a very simple way, and is therefore an excellent introduction to many classic card games they will play when they are older.

Number of Players: 4+, best with 6+.

Age Range: 6+

Type of Game / Skills: Luck

Cards: Standard deck of 52 cards. Aces are high.

Aim: To win the most "tricks"

Instructions: Deal the cards evenly face down to each player and include one extra "dummy" hand. Any extra cards go into the "dummy", which is placed face down in the centre of the table, but closest to the player on the dealer's left. Players don't look at their cards but place them face down in front of them.

The player left of the dealer turns over the top card of the "dummy" and calls out the suit for "trumps" (see below). Then he turns over the top card on his pile and calls it out. Now everyone else turns over their cards at once and looks to see if they have "beaten" player 1's card, by having a higher card in the same suit, or any card in the trump suit. A card in the "trump" suit always trumps – or beats – a card in the lead suit. If there is more than one card in the trump suit, the higher trump wins. A card in a different suit to the lead that is not in the trump suit will never win.

Whoever wins the "trick" gathers up all the cards (including the "dummy" card) and places them, face down, in a stack in front of him (separate from his face down pile). As more tricks are won they are stacked on top but at angles to keep them separate and make counting easy at the end.

The "dummy" is moved closer to the next player round to the left, who leads off the next round by turning over the top card and calling trumps, and then playing his card. It is a definite advantage to lead the round and, by moving the "dummy" each time, it helps to remember whose turn it is to lead.

Play continues until all rounds have been played, and then tricks are counted up.

Example round:

Player 1 turns over the top card and states "Clubs are trumps." He then turns over his card and states "10 of Spades". Player 2 has the King of Hearts, Player 3 the 5 of Spades, Player 4 the 9 of Diamonds, Player 5 the 2 of Clubs and Player 6 the Jack of Spades. Player 5 wins the trick.

Oh Hell

My father used to love this game but as a child I found it rather stressful in case I made a silly "promise" which I couldn't fulfil! Don't let that put you off as it's a very good game, a great step towards learning the ins and outs of tricks and trumps, and plays well with a group of up to seven. You might prefer the names "Oh Well" or "I Promise".

Number of Players: 3 to 7

Age Range: 8+

Type of Game / Skills: Tricks & trumps

Cards: Standard deck of 52 cards. Paper and pencil for scoring needed. Aces are high.

Aim: To win with the highest score

Instructions: Cut the cards to decide which suit will be "Trumps" for the round, then deal out the whole pack (putting aside any spare cards until the next round if you don't have 4 players).

Players study their cards and decide how many tricks they think they can win, or "make", with their hand, bearing in mind the Trumps suit. They then announce "I will make four tricks" – or whatever they think, and the dealer writes the promises down.

The player to the dealer's left begins by leading a card, and the other players either follow suit, trump (with a chance of winning), or throw away another suit (no chance of winning). As always, the highest card in the lead suit, or the highest trump, wins the trick, and the winner takes the cards and stacks them in front of him. The winner of the trick starts the next by leading another card from his hand.

At the end of the round, tricks are counted up and compared against original promises. If you matched your promise, you get the number of tricks you made plus a bonus of 10. Otherwise you score -1 for each trick over or under your promise. The highest score after a number of rounds, or the first person to reach 100, is the winner.

Knockout Whist

Many of the whist games are hard for children to grasp, but knockout whist is simple enough, and goes quickly enough, to be enjoyable for a group of kids or a family to play. Use your judgement, as some children may not appreciate being "knocked out" of the game!

Number of Players: 2 to 7

Age Range: 8+

Type of Game / Skills: Tricks & trumps

Cards: Standard deck of 52 cards. Aces are high.

Aim: To win as many tricks as possible and avoid being knocked out.

Instructions: Deal seven cards to each player and put the remaining cards in a stack to the side, turning the top card over to declare "Trumps".

Players sort out their cards into suits and ranks. The player to the dealer's left leads the first card, and other players follow suit if they can, or trump (in an effort to win). If they can do neither they should throw away a low value card. As always, the highest card in the lead suit, or the highest trump, wins the trick, and the winner takes the cards and stacks them in front of him. The winner of the trick starts the next by leading a card from his hand.

When all the tricks have been made, anyone who didn't win at least one trick drops out. If one player wins all seven tricks, then he wins the game.

Otherwise, the cards are gathered up and shuffled, and this time 6 cards are dealt out and 6 tricks played with a new Trumps suit– and so on, until each remaining player is only dealt 1 card and the winner of the final trick is the overall winner!

Cheat

Also known as "I Doubt It" this is a very popular game for children of a certain age (I'm thinking of young teenage boys in particular) but the older members of the family might prefer to avoid it!

Number of Players: 3+, better with more

Age Range: 8+

Type of Game / Skills: Luck, poker face

Cards: Standard deck of 52 cards for 3 or 4 players, two decks for 5 or more players.

Aim: To get rid of all your cards

Instructions: Deal out all the cards face down and give the players time to sort out their cards by rank.

The player to the dealer's left now puts from one to four cards onto the table, face down, stating a certain number of Aces. The next players puts down from one to four cards, stating a certain number of twos. Play continues with each player putting down from one to four cards of the next number in sequence – threes, fours, fives, and so on, all the way up to Kings.

Not everyone will have the cards that they are claiming to put down! The first player may not have any Aces. If she doesn't, she will have to brazen it out and put down some other card or cards, declaring "One Ace", "Two Aces" or whatever she chooses. If another player happens to know or suspect that she doesn't have what she claims to have, he can challenge her by saying "Cheat!" Her card or cards are turned over and if the doubter was right, she must take them back. If he was wrong, he has to take the cards.

Of course if two packs are being used, a player can put down between one and eight cards in each turn.

Given that the aim of the game is to get rid of all your cards, the more successful, sincere and sneaky you are at putting your cards down on the table, the more likely you are to win! Look carefully at the number of cards that a player puts on the table. In Cheat anything goes, and it has been known for one member of my family to give away 7 or 8 cards at a time while declaring only 3 or 4!

Knock

I learned this game from a friend at school (we called it Peanuckle) and introduced it to my family in my teenage years. It became a firm favourite and we have played it many, many times since. It breaks the ice with new friends and works very well as a multi-generation game. Play the first round or two gently to let everyone get a feel for the game, and then speed up and throw a "penalty" or two for mistakes and slow play to liven things up! Or just play it at a "serious" card game – you'll still enjoy it.

Number of Players: 3+, best with more

Age Range: 8+

Type of Game / Skills: Noisy

Cards: Two decks of cards for uninterrupted play.

Aim: To get rid of all your cards (and have the highest score in a multi-round game).

Instructions: Deal seven cards to each player, face down. The rest of the pack is placed face down in the centre, and the top card turned over to form a face up pile next to the pack. Players should sort their cards by suit.

The player to the left of the dealer goes first, by placing a card or cards onto the face-up pile which matches the face-up card by rank or suit if he can. If he can't, he takes a card from the pack.

Obviously with the aim to get rid of all your cards, the more cards you put down and the fewer cards you pick up, the better. There are a number of special cards that make the game fun which I explain below.

When you have only two cards left in your hand, you must knock on the table (or shout "Peanuckle!") to alert the other players – before the next player plays his card. When a player puts down his last card the game is over, and the other players count their cards and give themselves a minus score. The player who went out gets a positive score of 5.

Special cards: Certain cards in the pack have an extra role to play, as follows:

2: If a player puts down a 2, the next player cannot put down but instead must pick up 2 from the pack – unless he can put down a 2 too. If he can, the next player must pick up 4 – unless he can put down a 2 and make the next player pick up 6 – and so on. With a two pack game the worst case scenario (thankfully very rare) is that a player has to pick up 16 cards!

3: 3s work the same as 2s, but are just that little bit more painful if you are on the receiving end of a few of them in a row!

7: If a player puts down a 7, he places another card on top immediately, of any rank or suit. You can follow a 7 with another 7 and another 7 (and so on) before then putting whatever you like on top. They are a great way of getting rid of cards and changing the suit in your favour.

8: If a player puts down an 8, the next person in line misses a go.

J: If a player puts down a Jack, the order of play changes in the opposite direction. As you've started clockwise, the first Jack will change the direction anti-clockwise.

Penalties: Once you get the hang of the game, penalties make Knock more fun. It is possible that with an all-child game they could cause arguments but in our experience in mixed games they instead cause much hilarity and are taken well. Obviously it is best to aim the penalties at older players more and give younger children more slack!

Award a penalty of one card from the pack for a player who hesitates too long before making their move, or who puts down the wrong card. Award a similar penalty for someone who plays when they shouldn't, perhaps when their turn has just been missed because of an 8 or a Jack being played by the previous player – or when they just aren't concentrating! Award a penalty of two cards from the pack for someone who forgets to "knock" when they have only 2 cards left in their hand.

Use your discretion - but you might also consider awarding a penalty to an older player who keeps forgetting the role of the special cards or is taking too long to organise their hand after a big pick-up – or perhaps to someone who is enjoying someone else's misfortune too much!

Example Game (4 players):

Player 1 deals and turns up Ace of Hearts.

Player 2 puts down 5 of Hearts

Player 3 places 7 of Hearts followed by Jack of Diamonds

Player 4 puts down 10 of Diamonds. Penalty card awarded! The game has been reversed and it was not Player 4's turn.

Player 2 puts down 3 of Diamonds

Player 1 puts down 3 of Spades

Player 4 picks up 6 cards!

Player 3 puts down Jack of Spades

Pause

Player 4 is awarded another penalty card for failing to notice that the direction of the game has been reversed again and it was his turn!

And so on...

Variations:

Extra special cards: You can add in more special cards to make the game sillier. Examples that we have played are:

K: When a King is played everyone has to stand until another "royal" card is put down on the table.

A: When a player puts down an Ace they have to get up and run around the table, being back in their place and ready to play for their next turn. This can be tricky if the player to go next happens to have a Jack, or if everybody works fast!

Newmarket

Newmarket is an exciting game and very easy to learn, but we found that the addition of a "dummy" hand made it more suitable for a slightly older age group. It is an excellent game for large family gatherings.

Number of Players: 3 to 8

Age Range: 8+

Type of Game / Skills: Simple strategy

Cards: One deck of cards plus the Ace of Hearts, King of Clubs, Queen of Diamonds and Jack of Spades from a second deck. You will also need at least 10 counters per person.

Aim: To win the most counters.

Instructions: Deal out the cards, but deal an extra "dummy" hand as well. Place the four extra cards from the second deck face up in the middle of the table, where they will stay throughout the game. Divide up the counters and give an equal amount to each player.

Before play begins, each player puts one counter on each of the four cards in the middle of the table. Everyone looks at their hands and the dealer decides whether he is happy with his. If not, he can exchange it for the "dummy" hand and put his hand aside. If he does not want the "dummy" hand, he auctions it to the other players, who bid for it with their counters and exchange their hand, paying the dealer, if they win. If no-one wants the "dummy", leave it aside.

Play now begins. The player to the left of the dealer puts down the lowest card of any suit in his hand, saying the name out loud (eg "2 of Spades"). In this game, Aces are the highest cards. Whoever has the next card up in the same suit (in this case 3 of Spades) puts it down, saying the name. Play continues in this way as far as it can. If you put down one of the four cards in the centre of the table, you collect the counters on top. Sometimes the next card in the sequence will be in the "dummy". This is called a "stop".

When the sequence is "stopped", the player who put the last card down starts a new sequence with her lowest card in a suit of the other colour.

If she has no appropriate card, the player to her left starts the sequence off. If a sequence goes all the way up to the Ace of the suit, the player who puts down the Ace starts off the next sequence in the same way.

The first player to put down all his cards collects a counter from each player as a reward, and another hand is dealt.

Sixteen

This is a good game for a large group of children or a mixed age group. Some addition skills will be necessary! It has similarities with Pontoon (page 96) and introduces a "banker".

Number of Players: 4 to 10

Age Range: 8+

Type of Game / Skills: Addition skills needed

Cards: One deck of cards from which you remove the eights and sixes, except the Six of Hearts. Court cards count 10. Aces count 1. The other cards count their face value. You will need a large stack of counters, divided equally between the players.

Aim: To win the most counters.

Instructions: Place the cards face down in the centre of the table and have each player pick one, then compare to find the lowest. If two players have the same low card use Bridge ranking (Spades, Hearts, Diamonds, Clubs) to choose the lowest. For a smaller group it might be quicker to "cut" the cards – that is, the cards are placed in one stack face down and each player in turn picks up a section of the pack and turns the section over to see the card on the bottom, before replacing the cards for the next person to "cut".

The player who picked the lowest card is declared the banker for the round, or for the game. She shuffles the cards and places the whole pack face down in front of the player to her left.

That player now picks up one card and looks at it, keeping it hidden from everyone else. The aim is to hold two cards in your hand (no more than two) which add up to 16. The player now picks up a second card and adds up the total. If he has over 16 he is "bust" and must stop. If he has less than a total of 16 he can pick up one more card and choose one of the two already in his hand to discard, face down.

The player should try not to give away what his total is to other players. They will not know whether he is stopping because he has a good number or has gone bust.

When all players have taken their turn (except the banker), the banker asks everyone to turn over their cards and place them place up on the table.

Players who have exactly 16 get paid by the banker, one counter for every player in the game. So if there are 8 players the banker must pay 8 counters to everyone who gets exactly 16.

If a player reaches exactly 16 and also holds the Six of Hearts, not only does the banker pay him, but every player must give him two counters.

A player who has gone "bust" pays the banker one counter for every digit over 16. So if his cards total 20, he owes the banker 4. Players who have less than 16 pay one counter to the banker.

Example round:

Player 1 picks up a 10, then a 2 (10 + 2 = 12). She decides to pick up another card, which is a 4. She discards the 2 (10 + 4 = 14) and stops.

Player 2 picks up a King, and then a Jack. He is bust, to he stops.

Player 3 picks up a 10 and the Six of Hearts. She stops.

Player 4 picks up a Jack and a 5. He stops.

The players turn their cards over. The banker pays 3 counters to player 3, who achieved 16. Players 1, 2 and 4 give 2 counters to player 3 because she held the Six of Hearts. Player 2 gives the banker 4 counters. Players 1 and 4 gives the banker 1 counter.

Variations:

Allow two or even three new cards to be taken, as long as one from the existing hand is discarded each time (not the card that has just been picked up).

For younger children, play the whole hand with cards face up on the table. Many children enjoy going "bust"!

German Whist

This two-player game is simple enough for children to learn quickly, but challenging and competitive enough to keep them playing! You don't require a lot of space to play so it makes a great game for an airplane or train journey.

Number of Players: 2

Age Range: 8+

Type of Game / Skills: Tricks, strategy

Cards: One standard deck of cards. You will need pencil and paper for scoring.

Aim: To win the most tricks.

Instructions: Deal 13 cards to each player and put the remainder of the pack face down in the centre of the table. Turn the top card face up. That card's suit becomes "Trumps" for this whole round of the game.

There are two parts to the game. In the first part, Player 1 (not the dealer) leads a card, and Player

2 *follows suit* (that is, puts down another card in the same suit). If they can't follow suit they can either throw down another card in a different suit, and lose the trick, or put down a card from the Trump suit and win the trick.

The winner of the "trick" takes the top, exposed card from the stack, and puts it into his hand. The other player takes the next card down, and then turns over the top card again. The cards from the trick itself are put aside and are no longer important. Play continues in this way until all the cards in the stack have been taken.

Now part 2 of the game begins. Whoever won the last trick in part 1 leads the first card, and again the next player must follow suit if possible, trump, or throw away. Now each trick is stacked in front of the winning player to be counted at the end. The winner of the trick leads the next trick, and all 13 tricks are played.

Tricks from part 2 are counted up and the winner subtracts 6 from his total to get his score. If he won 10 tricks, for example, his score for the round would be 4.

Strategy: The object in part 1 is to get the best cards you can in order to take the most tricks in part 2. The first exposed card is valuable because it is a trump, so it is important to try to win that first trick. After that, players must look at the exposed card each time and decide whether they want to try to win it, or try not to win! And of course your opponent is thinking along the same lines as you...

Casino

The instructions for Casino sound complicated but it's actually a relatively simple game –and a fun one, too, which children enjoy.

Number of Players: 2

Age Range: 8+

Type of Game / Skills: Strategy

Cards: One standard deck of cards. You will need pencil and paper for scoring.

Aim: To win with the highest score.

Instructions: The object of the game is to win the most cards, using the various strategies explained below, and to score points for doing so.

Scoring: When you win certain cards they win you extra points, as follows:

- Ten of Diamonds (Great Casino) – 2 points
- Two of Spades (Little Casino) – 2 points

- Aces – 1 point
- Player with the most cards – 3 points
- Player with the most spades – 2 points
- Sweeps (explained below – 1 point each

Play: Deal four cards to each player and four more face up in the centre of the table, in a row. Put the stack aside. When both players have played their four cards, four more are dealt to each (but not to the table). On each turn, a player tries to "win" as many cards as he can, with particular emphasis on winning scoring cards. There are various ways he can play.

1. **Pairing**: If he has a card in his hand which matches a card or cards on the table, he can "win" them. He can pair with Court cards, but only win one card at a time.

To "win" cards, he puts the relevant card from his hand down on the table and then takes the card(s) from the layout, stacking them all to one side in front of him.

1. **Combine:** If two or more cards on the table add up to the same number as one card in his hand, he can "win" them. If there was a 4, 5, 6

and 3 on the table, he could win all of them with one 9 in his hand.

2. Building: He can take one card from his hand and place it with one on the table, to build up to a total which matches a card in his hand. For example, he could place a 2 on top of a 5 on the table, saying "Building Seven", as long as he had a 7 in his hand ready to win them with on his next go, and assuming his opponent hadn't already won the cards. If, on his next go, there was another 7 on the table, he could win that too.

If a player begins a build on one turn, he must complete the build on his next turn if his opponent hasn't snatched it away.

4. **Increase a build**: When one player has built, the other player can add to the build. In the example above, the second player could add an Ace and declare "Building Eight".

3. Trailing: A player must take cards from the table or build if he can. If he can't, he must "trail" – that is, put one of his cards down into the centre.

Sweeps: If a player wins all the cards in the centre in one turn, or wins the last remaining card in the centre, he scores 1 point. The easiest way to remember to score sweeps is to turn one card from his pile over for every sweep scored.

Play ends when all cards have been played. Any cards which are left in the centre are added to the pile of the last player to take cards in, and scores are totted up.

Variations:

Royal Casino: The Court cards count as follows: Jack 11, Queen 12, King 13. The Ace counts either 1 or 14 – you decide when you play it. You can match and win more than one Court card at a time.

Draw Casino: When the first cards have been dealt the remainder are placed to the side as a draw pile. After each play a new card is taken from the pile. When all cards have been drawn, continue until the remaining cards have been played.

Greek Casino

As you might guess from the name, this game has elements of Casino in it. You can play Greek Casino with up to eight people and I think it's a little easier, and a bit more fun!

Number of Players: 2 to 10

Age Range: 8+

Type of Game / Skills: Strategy

Cards: One standard deck of cards for up to 6 players, two shuffled together for more. You will need pencil and paper for scoring.

Aim: To win with the highest score.

Instructions: Deal six cards to each player, and then put four cards face up in one pile in the centre of the table. Put the rest of the cards aside for the next deal.

The player to the left of the dealer plays first, placing a card from his hand onto the top of the face-up stack. If he can match the card on top, he takes the stack and puts them face down in front of him. If he can't, he places any card on top and play passes to the left.

If the stack has been taken, Player 2 has no choice but to put a new card down, face up, to form the new stack. Otherwise he tries to match the top card if he can.

Tenners: If there is only one card on the stack when it is matched, the stack is won with a bonus of 10 points. The easiest way to remember is to place is sideways in your pile.

Aces: An Ace takes the pack whenever it is placed, regardless of the card beneath it. Save them and play them strategically for a bigger score!

When all players have used the cards in their hand, another 6 cards are dealt, and 4 more cards added to the stack.

When there aren't enough cards left for a fresh deal, each player scores his pile as follows:

- Ten of Diamonds (Great Casino) – 2 points
- Two of Spades (Little Casino) – 2 points

- Aces – 1 point
- Player with the most cards – 3 points
- Player with the most spades – 2 points
- Every tenner won – 10 points

Rummy

There are many variations to Rummy – and that's because it is a great game for all ages, and can be played with 2 or a small group just as successfully! Rummy is almost certainly based on the Chinese game of Mah-jong.

Number of Players: 2 to 6

Age Range: 8+

Type of Game / Skills: Strategy

Cards: One standard deck of cards. You will need pencil and paper for scoring.

Aim: To win with the highest score.

Instructions: Deal 7 cards to each player. The remaining cards are placed face down in the centre as a stack, and the top card is turned up and placed next to it to start the discard pile. If at any time during the game the stack runs out, turn the discard pile over and start again.

The object of the game is to match up your cards into three or four of a kind (three Kings, four 2s etc) or runs (at least 3 cards in sequence in the same suit, such as 8, 9 and 10 of Hearts). These groupings are known as "melds" Before the game starts, players should arrange their cards accordingly.

Every turn starts with a player picking up a card, either from the top of the pack (unseen) or from the top of the discard pile. She can then make "melds" if she chooses, in which case she puts down her melds – at least three cards in each – on the table face up in front of her. They will count towards her score. She doesn't have to place a meld, but can keep it hidden in her hand. Finally, she declares the end of her go by discarding a card (choosing the least important card from her hand and putting it face up on the top of the discard pile).

At the beginning of the game it is normal for players to pick up, rearrange their cards a little, and then discard, as they try to build melds, but soon players will start to put their melds onto the table. Once melds are down, opponents can build on them. For example, if Player 1 has put down 3 of Hearts, 3 of Diamonds and 3 of Clubs in one meld, Player 2 could put down 3 of Spades on his turn, keeping it in front of him so that it counts towards his score.

Remember, all turns must start by drawing a card and end by discarding a card. The exception is a winning turn, when a player puts down all his remaining cards onto the table and "goes out". He could also go out by putting down all but one of his cards, and discarding the last one.

Either way, that round is over and scores are totted up. Losing players count up the total points from the cards left in their hands: Court cards are 10 points each, Aces are 1 point each, and the other cards have their face value. These totals are added up and given to the winner.

Going Rummy: If a player manages to "go out" before any other player has put down cards on the table, he goes Rummy. He's going to get a great score anyway because his opponents will still have lots of cards in their hands – but in this case the score is doubled as well!

500 Rummy

500 Rummy differs from standard Rummy in that your melds score for you, as well as going out. You can play with up to eight. This was my family's favourite version of rummy, and we played it often. Somehow trying to decide whether to pick up the discard pile makes the game more fun!

Number of Players: 3 to 6

Age Range: 8+

Type of Game / Skills: Strategy

Cards: One standard deck of cards. You will need pencil and paper for scoring.

Aim: To win with the highest score.

Instructions: Deal seven cards to each player and play as for standard rummy. Instead of placing all discards on top of each other, however, you should spread them slightly so that all cards can be seen.

When it is your turn to pick up a card, you may choose a card from anywhere within the discard pile – as long as you can use that particular card straight away to put a meld on the table. You must then pick up every card above it in the pile as well.

When someone goes out, score your cards. Add up the value of your cards on the table and subtract the value of cards left in your hand. You get 15 points for every Ace unless it is the low card in a sequence of A-2-3, in which case it scores 1. Court cards count 10 each. Other cards count at face value. Whoever "goes out" gets an extra 15 points bonus, doubled to 30 points if they managed a "Rummy".

Obviously you should try to meld your higher value cards and not hold onto cards in your hand any longer than necessary, as they will count against you when someone goes out.

Tonk

Tonk is yet another variation of rummy. It's exciting and is best played at quite a fast pace.

Number of Players: 2 to 6

Age Range: 8+

Type of Game / Skills: Strategy

Cards: One standard deck of cards. You will need pencil and paper for scoring.

Aim: To win with the lowest score.

Instructions: Deal seven cards to each player and continue as in Rummy.

Tonk varies as follows.

Wild two's: Two's are wild and one (but not two) may be used in any meld when you don't have the right card.

Tonking: To "go out" you don't need to meld all your cards, as long as the remaining cards in your hand score 5 or less. Aces are low. You

87

don't go out immediately: when it is your turn, instead of picking up, melding and discarding, you simply announce "Tonk" and do nothing else. Your opponents now try to get as many cards out of their hands onto the table as possible before play returns to you, and you put your hand down on the table.

Scoring: The Tonker scores zero. The other players total up the count of the cards in their hands. The lowest score after a number of rounds wins.

Hearts

Hearts is another trick-playing game with an added twist that challenges all ages. It is a very popular family game but I have found it best played with older children.

Number of Players: 2 to 6, best with 4

Age Range: 10+

Type of Game / Skills: Tricks & trumps, strategy

Cards: One standard deck of cards. You will need a paper and pencil for scoring.

Aim: Avoid winning any tricks with hearts in them – or, alternatively, win all 13 hearts! To have the lowest score at the end of the game.

Instructions: Deal the pack out as follows:

- With 3 players, discard one 2
- With 4 players, deal the whole pack
- With 5 players, discard two 2s
- With 6 players, discard four 2s
- With 7 players, discard three 2s.

The player to the dealer's left begins by leading one of his cards, and other players either follow suit. There are no trumps so the trick is won by the highest card in the lead suit. The winner of the trick leads the next.

When all tricks have been played, each player examines his tricks for Hearts. For each Heart score 1. If one player has all the hearts, he scores zero and all the other players score 5. The player with the lowest score after a number of rounds wins.

Calamity Jane

This game is similar to Hearts and is also known as Black Lady. Many people actually refer to this game as Hearts, just to confuse matters. It has a horrible twist to it – the pass - that children enjoy enormously, especially when they have a parent sitting to their left!

Number of Players: 3 to 7, best with 4

Age Range: 10+

Type of Game / Skills: Tricks & trumps, strategy

Cards: One standard deck of cards. You will need a paper and pencil for scoring.

Aim: Avoid winning any tricks with hearts in them and avoid taking the Queen of Spades (Calamity Jane). Alternatively, win all 13 hearts and Calamity Jane! To have the lowest score at the end of the game.

Instructions: Deal the pack out as follows:

- With 3 players, discard one 2

- With 4 players, deal the whole pack
- With 5 players, discard two 2s
- With 6 players, discard four 2s
- With 7 players, discard three 2s.

Players look at their cards and decide on three that they don't want to play. All players put their three cards on the table and then pass them to the player on their left, picking up the cards passed to them by the player on their right.

Play continues as in Hearts, although in this game you want to avoid the Queen of Spades as well as the hearts.

To score, count 1 point for every heart and a frightening 13 for Calamity Jane! The player with the lowest score after a number of rounds wins.

Racing Demon

I spent many hours in my childhood playing this noisy frantic game – a mad version of patience, really - and loved it. It's not for the timid and shy! You need a lot of space – a large floor is best - and old packs of cards.

Number of Players: 2+

Age Range: 10+

Type of Game / Skills: Noisy, fast

Cards: One old deck of cards per player, preferably with different banks for easier sorting later

Aim: To get all your cards out first and have the highest score.

Instructions: Each player shuffles his pack and then deals four face-up cards in front of him for his "Layout". He holds the remaining stack in his hand, face down.

When one player shouts "go" the race begins. If you have an Ace in your Layout, move it into the centre as a "Foundation" card, and replace it with a new card from your hand. Once an Ace becomes a Foundation, anyone can start to build up on it with the next card in suit, all the way up to the King. Players should keep an eye out for Foundation opportunities and grab them quickly when they see them!

Your four Layout cards act as a holding pen – a way to get as many cards onto the table and ready to play as possible. You build downwards on them, alternating black and red cards. At any time that you manage to put a Layout card onto a Foundation card, replace it with a new card from your stack. When you've made all the moves you can with your four Layout cards, start to use your stack as follows:

Count three cards. Turn them over and put them down on the table face up. Look at the top card. Can you do anything with it? Can you move it to the Foundation, or your Layout? If so, you can look at the card beneath it. If not, count another three cards, turn them over and put them down on the table, look at the top card – and so on.

When you get to the bottom of your stack, pick up the face up pile from the table, turn it over and start again.

Work as quickly as you can. As soon as someone gets all their cards out the game is over. All the cards already placed onto Foundation cards in the centre are sorted out and counted, and a winner declared.

Variation:

Racing Demon is also played using the traditional Klondike patience layout.

Pontoon

Also known as Vingt-et-un, Twenty-One and Black Jack, this is of course a well-known casino gambling game (with some slight variations). Although my explanation is long the game is relatively simple to grasp and it works especially well for a large group of older children and teenagers of mixed ages, played with counters.

Number of Players: 4 to 10. One player starts as banker (an advantage).

Age Range: 10+

Type of Game / Skils: Concentration helps. Some players might like to try to count cards and work out odds

Cards: Two decks of cards. Give each player an equal number of counters.

Aim: To reach a point value of 21 but no more, beating the banker's point value. To win the most counters.

Point Values: Court cards count as 10. An Ace in a player's hand can count either 1 or 11. An Ace in the banker's hand always counts 11. The other cards count according to face value.

Instructions: The banker gives each player and himself one card, face down. Players look at their cards and "bet" by putting at least one counter in front of them to play, or more if they think they have a good card. When all bets are placed the banker looks at his card and has the right to "double" – in which case everyone has to double their bets.

The banker then gives everyone another card, face down. Again players look at their cards, and if someone has a pair he may at this point decide to "split" his cards and play two hands. He places the cards side-by-side and stakes the same bet on the second card as on his original card, and the banker gives him another card on top of each.

Now the banker looks at his cards. If he has a "Natural" – an Ace and a Court card or 10, he turns his cards face up and everyone pays him double what they bet (unless a player also has a

Natural – see below). The hands are thrown in and another round is dealt.

Assuming the banker doesn't have a "Natural", he asks the players if they have one. If a player does, the banker pays him double his stake and after this round the bank passes to him. If more than one player has a Natural, the bank always passes to the player nearest the banker's left.

The banker now turns to each player, starting with the one on his left, and asks them if they want more cards. A player can choose one of three options:

To stick: his existing two cards are close enough to 21 to prevent him risking another card, and more than 15. When sticking it is traditional to stack your cards face down in front of you and put your bet on top of them.

To buy: He asks for another card, paying for it with a number of counters not more than his original stake. The new card is given to him face down.

To twist: He asks for another card, which is given to him face up.

He continues to buy or twist until he either sticks, goes bust (his count is over 21), or has 5 cards totalling under 21. He can't receive more than 5 cards. In addition, once he has asked to twist, he cannot buy. If he has bought, however, he can twist his next card.

If a player goes bust, he turns his cards face up and hands his stake to the banker.

When all players have played their hands and have either gone bust or are sticking, the banker turns his cards over and gives himself more if he wants. If he goes bust he pays everyone still in the game, matching their stake. But if he sticks he can announce that he is "paying higher scores", in which case anyone with the same or lower score as the banker will have to pay him. See the example game overleaf.

Example Game (5 players):

Deal 1 (after which Players bet):

Player 1 is dealt Ace of Spades and bets 3 counters

Player 2 is dealt 4 of Hearts and bets 1 counter

Player 3 is dealt 10 of Hearts and bets 4 counters

Player 4 is dealt 6 of Clubs and bets 1 counter

Banker deals himself the Jack of Diamonds. This is a good card so he decides to "double", and all the players have to double their bets.

Deal 2:

Player 1 now holds Ace of Spades and King of Clubs

Player 2 now holds 4 of Hearts and 5 of Spades

Player 3 now holds 10 of Hearts and 8 of Hearts

Player 4 now holds 6 of Clubs and 6 of Spades

Banker now holds Jack of Diamonds and 7 of Diamonds

Play begins:

Players look at their cards. Player 4 could double but decides the 6 isn't good enough.

Banker looks at his own cards. He has no Natural.

Banker asks players if they have a Natural. Player 1 shows his, and banker pays him 12 counters (double his doubled stake). At the end of this round Player 1 will become banker.

Banker asks Player 2 if he wants cards. He twists and receives the 9 of Diamonds, giving him a total of 17. He sticks.

Banker turns to Player 3 and can see by the way he has placed his cards that he is sticking.

Banker asks Player 4 if he wants cards. Player 4 "buys for 2" – that is, he adds 2 counters to his pile and receives a face down card. It is the Queen of Clubs and Player 4 is bust. He gives his 3 counters to the banker.

Banker turns his cards over and sees that he has 17. He says "I will pay 18".

Player 2 pays the banker 2 counters.

Player 3 receives 8 counters from the banker.

About the Author

Lindsay Small is the creator and owner of www.ActivityVillage.co.uk, a UK website which has helped parents, grandparents and teachers keep kids busy since 2000 with thousands of free colouring pages, puzzles, worksheets and printable activities as well as an enormous collection of craft ideas and games. Activity Village has well over a million visitors each month.

Lindsay, together with her brother Robin Hammond, was the first to produce a book of Sudoku puzzles especially for kids.

Made in the USA
Monee, IL
11 November 2019